# JOHNNY'S WORLD
## *The Final Chapter*

# JOHNNY'S WORLD

## THE FINAL CHAPTER

J.W. SANGWIN

Charleston, SC
www.PalmettoPublishing.com


*Johnny's World: The Final Chapter*
Copyright © 2023 by J.W. Sangwin



First Edition


Paperback ISBN: 979-8-8229-2026-2
eBook ISBN: 979-8-8229-2079-8

Well, just as I thought
I was finished with the series…

Here's
***The Final Chapter***

# Introduction

Hello again! Nate Thomas back with a look at what life was like without our good friend Johnny Sampson. No, life was not hopeless. The future continued to lie ahead. Even without Johnny in it, Johnny's World existed, and we were determined to prove it!

# THE FINAL CHAPTER

Each of us who were considered part of Johnny's World took the day after the memorial service to meditate and allow all we had experienced to sink in a bit. Yes, I admit that it was a fact that we had lost a particularly important part of our lives. We would never see him or hear his spoken voice again. One thing was for certain, would forever hear him say, "Hey, Tin-Man."

A couple of days after the funeral, we were still at Mom and Dad's. I decided to take my old bike out for a spin. It was still in good enough condition for riding as long as I didn't race or pop a wheelie. I wanted to do some reminiscing.

Once again, down past our block was the corner store, but the name had been changed to Nguyen's Quick Stop, and I am quite sure it wasn't any quicker.

As I came to the next street, to my surprise, there was the old Miller house, still painted in almost every color imaginable.

* * *

In the next block came a sudden rush of tears and memories galore. It was fire station # 5, with those fire trucks that were as shiny and new looking as that first day I rode by. What especially touched my heart was a plaque hanging by that # 5. It said:

> *In memory of our most courageous firefighter, Johnny Christopher Sampson, who gave his life while saving others. Sister station #5, Louisville, Kentucky -June 4, 1987.*

I immediately did as I had done before. I turned around to head home, only to see the same two friends, Bruce, and Walter, walking along the sidewalk. I did as I had done then. I honked my horn, and instead of that loud, high-pitched sound, it sounded more like Walter's bird-of-prey. Bruce remarked, "Hey, man, did you steal Walter's bird's voice?" At that comment we all laughed.

It seemed like yesterday that we, the gang of Johnny's World, were just beginning our adventures together, and much like that very last time when I took a moment to reflect.

That afternoon was spent remembering and laughing about the good times us four, and of course the rest of our gang, had. We all had to get back to our regular lives, so we said our good-byes and went our separate ways, for now.

* * *

The drive back home didn't take but an hour and a half. Yes, a few years ago, I had received an opportunity to go teach at a small university in our part of the state, about ninety miles from Appleton. It would mean moving from friends and relations. Mom was still in Appleton. She had retired from teaching. One day prior to our final decision to accept the offer, I went by for a visit. "Okay, Tinsley Nathaniel…what's bothering you?" I knew she knew a serious matter was about to be discussed. After I shared some details, she said as only she could, "Tinsley, as I have said before, pray for direction and follow your heart. You won't go wrong when you trust in the Lord!" The next thing I knew I had to do, besides praying was to call Johnny.

I knew it was a scheduled day off for Johnny, so when the phone rang about six times, I got concerned.

"Yello," Johnny answered. "Sampson's answering service!"

"Johnny, this is me, Tinsley Nathaniel," I said in a somewhat frantic voice.

"Oh, hey, Tin-Man! What's up?"

Seriously, I asked, "Where were you? The phone rang forever, and I got concerned."

"You knew this was a day off for me. I was outside at the neighbor's house. They have a boy named Joe who is ten years old. His dad is in the military overseas. I was playing catch with his football. He is a good kid, and I thought he might need someone. I know I am not his dad, but I can be a friend."

For a moment, I forgot why I had called.

I did eventually get to the reason I had called, and he did support my decision to take the position at the school, but I was once again amazed at what a devoted friend he could be.

* * *

Weeks after the funeral service, I was going through some stuff in our garage. They were storage bins from years back. One was marked *High School years*. I brought the bin in the house and sat at the dining table. Audrey was in a nearby room, so she came in and asked, "What is going on? What all is in that container?"

I explained that it was a bunch of things from our high school days. "I was curious, so I brought it in to see what kind of memories I might find." Audrey remarked, "Maybe you should fear some of it, you never know…out of sight, out of mind."

I had forgotten that Johnny had been notorious for having someone around taking pictures when you least expected it. So, it was on the day of tryouts for our high school football team. There were pictures of Audrey and Patricia Newberry and their girlfriends in the stands and on the sidelines. Included was a picture of when Johnny had thrown that pass to me right when Audrey had yelled, "Go Nate!" Naturally, I had looked toward her instead of keeping my eyes on the ball. There was the picture of me and my bloody nose and eventually bruised face. One such picture was of Walter when he had first spied his bird-of-prey. There was Walter, big eyed and mouth wide open. Actually, come to think of it, that was quite normal for Walter.

* * *

While looking through the bin, I came upon a group picture that I had taken that included Johnny's sister Ann and her eventual husband Bruce. It was rare to have a picture of Bruce, and come to think of it, we never really got to see Ann long enough for any picture taking. I recalled that on the day of Johnny's service,

Ann and Bruce had to leave immediately after the service at the church. Audrey told me that Ann thanked us for helping with the planning and all for the service, but they had to get back to the store. I couldn't help but wish things could have gone differently between her and her parents. Johnny told me one day, "My mom and dad keeps riding Ann so much about her spending too much time down at the corner store hanging around that Mayfield boy. They keep saying that no good will come from it. The only problem with that is that I am right in the middle of such a difficult situation that it strains our relationships. T-Man, my parents don't understand what true love does to a person when it is genuine, and I honestly believe that the love between those two is just that."

The only problem was that Ann never knew how Johnny felt about them, so it affected their relationship.

* * *

One thing about Johnny that everyone would agree with was that he kept his word and always seemed to have an eye to the future. I remembered the words he had said to me the day we moved to Appleton. His hand of friendship and the words "Can I help?" meant "Welcome to our life; you're now a part of it!"

From that very first day and every day after, Johnny Sampson had made sure this nerdy boy from the east was included. I remembered when I told him, "Johnny, I don't think they like me," referencing the neighborhood kids on that day.

"Oh, give them time, they'll come around," he assured me.

* * *

As I continued to look through the bin of memories, I saw this purple envelope with rainbows on it. It appeared to have never been opened. It was addressed to Carol and had Johnny's return address, but no stamp. I decided to open it, but I asked Audrey to be with me as I opened it.

Inside the colorful envelope was a birthday card with a letter in it. The card was a "Happy 21st Birthday" card. As I recalled, both Carol and Walter were born in February of the same year. Carol was thirteen days older than Walter. After Walter and Carol had started "dating", he would refer to himself as a "love child, since he was born on Valentines Day, he was destined for L-O-V-E." As I began to open the letter, I looked at Audrey and said, "Should I be doing this? I could just give the card and letter to Carol. After all, it is addressed to her."

Audrey quickly responded, "Nate, it was not mailed for some reason. Let's read it and see if we can figure out why." I opened the letter and began to read.

> *Dear Carol,*
>
> *On this your 21st birthday, I feel the need to tell you how wonderful a person you are and to apologize for the way we "friends" have treated you from time to time. You have been a great across-the-street neighbor forever, it seems, and I sometimes wonder if Walter has noticed you as he should. He appears to spend more time joking around and treating you as the punchline, as if he would even have to. It is very noticeable to me how you feel about him. You need to step it up and tell him the way it is. If you don't,*

*who knows what he may do. Enough said. I hope you
enjoy your birthday.*

*Your friend and matchmaker,*

*Johnny Sampson.*

"Oh, my! Audrey, if this had been mailed and Walter had found out, things might not have gone as they did. I am so glad Johnny changed his mind, but why didn't he destroy it?"

For one thing, I recalled us four guys, Johnny, Walter, Bruce, and myself, sitting around in our backyard around that time, talking about girls and our dating and plans, when suddenly, Walter had shocked us with "Oh, I almost forgot. Carol and I are getting married."

"When is this happening, and does Carol know?" I had asked.

Now I understood. "Audrey, I remember that right after Walter shared that information, Johnny jumped up suddenly and asked if he could be excused…something about needing to check his mail. He must have put it out to be picked up by the mail carrier, but there was no stamp on it."

Upon further examination of the envelope, I could see that a stamp had been removed. As I began to put the card and letter back in the envelope, I noticed that there was something else inside. It was a note that said,

*Tin-Man,*

*This just goes to show you that even I can misjudge
and goof up a good thing. Thank the Lord for His will
and interference.*

*Your eternal friend,*

*Johnny.*

All I could do at that was smile and give my wife the biggest hug.

*  *  *

The anticipation of a phone call can be pleasant when you know it will come eventually, but not at all when you realize it that will never happen again. It makes you regret the times you got that call and wished you hadn't answered. Good times bring good calls. Challenging times bring frustration and unrest. One such call had come about a year before Johnny's passing. The phone rang late one night, sometime before midnight. I had been doing some late-night typing and was preparing for bed. I let it ring for about three or four times, hoping that it might be a wrong number and that they would go away. I reluctantly answered, "Hello, Thomas residence?" I did not have caller ID.

It was Johnny calling from Louisville. "Tin-Man, this is Johnny. I am sorry to call so late. You know it is actually an hour later here. I just had to talk to someone. We had a run earlier that got pretty rough. It was an apartment fire that affected adjoining apartments. The fire began upfront but quickly spread toward the rear of the complex. The problem with the back apartments were that they had a fence directly behind them, which made it more difficult to access them without going all the way to the street and back around, so we had to call on another station unit to assist with the fire. This delayed our assessment of the rear apartment. By the time we contacted anyone back there, the apartment was fully engaged with fire. A family of five, which included a grandmother who had been bed/wheelchair bound for quite a while. The parents were able to get their two children safely out. The father went back in to try and rescue his mom but could not get past the inferno. He ended up with second and third degree burns on his arms, hands, and face. The grandmother was pronounced dead at the scene. Man, this one hit me hard. You know I spent a lot of time studying and researching fire prevention and about fire codes. This situation didn't have to have this result."

This was one of those times when I felt so inadequate. What could I tell or suggest that would help in this time of need? The only thing I could do was recite scripture that our pastors had shared in time of need. One such passage was found in 1 John 4.

"Johnny, the most important thing anyone can do is to make sure your main purpose for your actions is love. The Holy Spirit wants to help us share God's love in what we say and do. "Herein is our love made perfect, that we may have boldness…there is no fear in love…we love Him because He first loved us, so we must show that love." You are doing that every time you go on a run. Just make sure your heart is filled with that love and that your intentions are pure. Johnny, I have no doubt about your intentions. *Trust in God, and He will strengthen you!*"

After that conversation he didn't miss too many opportunities to thank me for encouraging him.

* * *

Once again, I found myself sitting at my desk, attempting to do some kind of creative writing that would be worthy to share with my students, when I suddenly recalled words spoken by my poetic friend Johnny Sampson: "When words fail to come and you just can't find them, perhaps the answer isn't found from Shakespeare or any theologian. Why not go and grab that pole and go to the hole and let that fish do the biting?" At that thought of wisdom, I arose from my desk and headed out the door, fishing gear in hand.

Yes, life in Johnny's World was much like a day of fishin'. Johnny always told me, "If you want to catch that big one, be patient; it will come to you just as sure as the weather changing." As I look back with fond memories, I can honestly say, **"All is right in Johnny's World!"**

# John W. Sangwin

The author of *Johnny's World: The Final Chapter* is J. W. Sangwin. This is the fifth and definitely, the final book in the series. John is married to Patricia Sangwin, and they reside in Port Arthur, Texas. John also has published *A Storybook Collection*. Please share these writings with others and always look on the positive side of life. Just remember: Jesus cares about you!